FREEDOM
IN
JOY

MY DESTINY IS NOT A MIRAGE

"Until now you have not asked for anything in my name. Ask and you will receive, and your joy will be complete."

John 16:24 (NIV)

Lavanda Rochelle Heard

MISSION
POSSIBLE
PRESS
Mission Possible Press, USA
Creating Legacies through Absolute Good Works
Extraordinary Living Series

The Mission is Possible.

Sharing love and wisdom for the young and "the young at heart," expanding minds, restoring kindness through good thoughts, feelings, and attitudes is our intent. May you thrive and be good in all you are and all you do…

Be Cause U.R. Absolute Good!

Published by
Mission Possible Press
A Division of Absolute Good
P.O. Box 8039, St. Louis, MO 63156
orders@absolutegood.com

ISBN 978-0-9852760-8-9

Dedication

To those of you who know there's more to life and feel like you might not be able to make it through another day. I know you can so continue to stand.

Love Notes

Paul (My Husband), you believe in me, you support me and you continue to love me no matter what. Thank you for staying with me through good and bad times. I simply love you.

Joshua and Joseph, thanks for putting up with your previously over-nurturing mom.

Mom (Alberta Holman), you remain my woman of faith. Thank you so much for living the life you walk and talk in love and strength. Pop (Bishop Levander Overton), though you are in heaven above, I sense your touch rest upon my heart and see your smiling face. Siblings - Theodore, Anthony, Demetrice, Eugene, Shirley, Marcus, Doralo, and Sis Julie (you're family too), thanks for the cute nicknames which helped propel me.

Bishop Geoffrey V. and Lady Glenda Dudley, thanks for being the spiritual life support for our family well-being.

Janet Greenlee, my YWCC Sponsor and Big Sister in Christ, thanks for assigning Psalm 34 to me when I was 14 years old.

Jo Ann Martin, thank you for showing me so much kindness. Your support and encouragement gave me freedom to examine my story and to tell it.

Jo Lena Johnson, from day one you have been my beacon of light. I am grateful and thankful to you for being so much more than my publisher. Your role in my life has been friend, coach, mentor, and prayer partner. Thanks for listening to my story, for never judging me but helping my voice to be heard.

Thanks to all whose names are not mentioned but know the role you played in my life.

"I bless GOD every chance I get; my lungs expand with his praise."

Psalm 34:1,
The Message Bible

Contents

Imprisonment or Freedom?
Thoughts and Feelings

*The way you see your future is more important than what
happened in the past. Focus forward.*

Chapter 1
A Top of the Arch View

Freedom in Joy is…Creating continuous moments of gratitude for each life experience.

We were not created as "beings" to "be" sitting idle. To move forward, you must be able to define what your purpose is, and have the mindset to move toward it, passing obstacles along the way. You must also establish a foundational connection in order to have the power, strength, wisdom and support of Spirit to carry you through. Every individual, including you and me, must find their own path to freedom and live in their destiny. I now move forward because I see the bigger picture. And so can you.

Change Your View

When you're standing at the base and looking up at the 630 foot Gateway Arch in St. Louis, Missouri, it's overwhelmingly big. When you're standing at the top of the Arch everything looks small below. The Arch is a great example of how perception works.

It wasn't until I changed my view, my thinking and how I saw what seemed to be gigantic in my life from a different perspective, that I realized I could choose to "be on top" of my situations or be conquered by them. When standing in the window, looking down over the city, everything looks small, including the Mississippi River. That's a good feeling.

Our circumstances and situations do not define who we are or what our purpose and destiny is. We must stand on top of them. See above them and not allow life to beat us down. We won't be carefree from the good and bad situations coming at us from every angle, but we can move forward through them and even rise above them. These experiences will inevitably make us stronger.

When we are at the level of our problems, circumstances, situations, we get overwhelmed, but when we rise above them, they are no longer giants to us. We must rise above them daily. We must go up in the elevator of our thoughts and mindset until we have conquered the obstacles and hindrances delaying us from walking into our destiny.

Chapter 2
Are You Free?

Position equates to power when you know where you are and are not.

If being free was easy, it wouldn't be worth much, would it? Freedom requires interdependence. You just can't separate some things. Your past, present and future are interrelated and cannot be separated. However, you can unglue them. Freedom, as it relates to interdependence means - awareness of your past, clarity on your present, and a workable plan to create and maintain your future.

This is your blueprint to gain freedom, and to stay free, through joy. Freedom In Joy is not just a catchy title, it's being aware of the thoughts and feelings which feed our minds and experiences every single day. In order to experience freedom, we must be willing to go beyond comfort, let go of some things, and also learn new things.

I Wasn't Free

Some of the toughest times are when we feel isolated and alone. Feeling alone is different than being alone. I've learned, there's always the hope of joy, but it took so long for me to really understand that. I had been stuck and afraid of change for most of my adult life. I thought surely no one else besides me feared the idea of change. I would cover up my emotions for fear of feeling rejection and having to deal with judgment calls. There were certain thoughts and experiences I did not want to address or talk about; however, I didn't really know how deeply other things were buried. I had my head in the sand, which was comfortable, since I didn't have to confront the situations which were holding me down. I was "acting up" as my personal development coach Jo Lena Johnson would call it. She would say, "Stop acting up," over and over again as we were strategizing and working through my issues. Primarily, recurring thoughts were causing me to act that away, holding back my marriage, my children, my life, my future and my destiny.

Having my coach as another voice was an interrupter of old patterns, serving as a consistent reminder to look up instead of acting up. Soul searching, I finally accepted the truth - I was acting up. I would never move forward unless I changed the way I looked at everything. *Why was I behaving this way?* I was so stuck in my head I would act like a little sad granny. Little stuff was messing me up. When I started letting it out, "it" was hard. These were things I had kept inside for so long because I didn't want to deal with them. I struggled, but I began to feel free because I was not burying anything anymore. I got real with myself - I knew if I didn't stop those thoughts and "stuff" I kept hidden inside, I was not going to be able to share and maybe even help someone else. When I got to the heart of the matter, I realized all that childhood fear was just pulling, blocking and sticking to me. I began feeling safe more moments than not, over time.

What About You?

Are you wandering in your thoughts and decision making? Are you wondering what your life purpose is? Do you know your purpose but have no idea how to fulfill it? Are you just going through the motions of an unfulfilled life? Do you feel like no one understands you or gets who you are? I found myself having to face these same questions. That's okay. Who you are matters, just as much as why you were born.

I have not always been an open person and found it difficult to trust. I felt that no one understood me because God reveals things to me. I also wondered if people would think I was crazy. I had to say, "No More!" This is who I am and it was time for me to step out and share with others.

The positives and negatives from the past happened and are still influencing the present, affecting how we think, behave, and go about our day-to-day life's journey. Without realizing it, many of us have allowed our negative life experiences from childhood to adulthood to harness our thoughts and decisions, thus dictating and determining the path we take. Sometimes the negativity blocks or stops us from walking into our God-intended destiny. It is not our circumstances and situations which define who we are and what path we should travel.

The Past Has Passed

Your reactions to the past may be holding you captive. Emotions can mess you up. What you still feel may have you stuck. What they did, didn't do, said, or didn't say - happened. Those are the facts. However, is your perspective worse than the reality of the past? The past has passed, stop being emotionally driven and let it go.

Creating New Thoughts

The past taught you what to think. Those thoughts have limited some of us. Negative thoughts took your freedom. New thoughts give it back. Sounds simple, it's not. Striving to live in your destiny requires you to learn how to think.

1. What are your primary thoughts about yourself, your life and your circumstances?

   Notice if each thought is mostly negative. If they are, this is an excellent time to begin to reshape the way you see your life.

2. What activities do you find positive and purposeful? When was the last time you participated in an uplifting and rewarding endeavor? What was it? Why did you do it? Why did you like it?

3. What new thought could you start to think about yourself that would affirm and uplift you?

I had to stop "acting up" and so can you. I'm not sad anymore nor defeated by fear. I'm free. I no longer feel guilt deep inside like I used to because I've addressed it. When things come up, I keep addressing them until they don't bind my mind, heart or future. I've been more transparent than ever as I've come to appreciate me as an individual. I don't feel embarrassed or ashamed with my issues. I keep working to do better, as I am overcoming my shortcomings. And so can you.

"Are you free?" If your answer is no, think about what situation, circumstance, emotion or habit is holding you captive. Working through this question will help you create the new thoughts you need to create your freedom and joy.

Creating New Self-Talk

Now that you have awareness and understanding of your thoughts, feelings, attitudes and behavior, it's time to change your thought process so your results (life) can change as well. Commit to your highest good. Make an earnest and sincere effort to create a new pattern of thinking and feeling. This means responding instead of reacting when things happen.

Self-Talk Examples:

When I see _____ I will _____ and keep moving.

When I hear _____ I will consider it and do_____ before replying.

When I feel _____ I will do _____.

I will forgive_____ so I can _____.

You know what's on your mind, so use these as examples and create some sentences which will work for you.

Creating New Activities

To get free, you must fill the space with new thoughts, leading to new emotions and new perspectives. You have a lot of choices, including working with a coach, a group, taking a class and/or reading and applying biblical principles. There's no one road to freedom, just get on the path!

Be soft on your past, it has passed. Be hard on your future, it's your desire and destiny. New thoughts take work, that's why "Joy" is part of the equation. Whenever you do something "in joy," it's good, causing you to want to move forward. Then you want more! Your thoughts never stop, so don't let your thoughts stop you.

By honestly examining ourselves, we gain an awareness of what is guiding and blocking our thoughts, perspective, and actions. After considering the "cost" of being bound to them, (wandering, pain, disease, low or scattered energy, bad attitude, incomplete projects, poor communication, difficult relationships…), accept they came for a reason.

Be grateful "it" happened and that "it" is over. "They" had enough control and it's time to lay them to rest. Write down, if necessary, circumstances and/or people to whom you've been giving control, revisiting those experiences for the last time. It happened. It was what it was. Literally say "thank you" to those experiences for giving you the chance to grow, however awkwardly, through them. Say goodbye to them, otherwise you risk going backward.

"You're what you are and where you are because of what's gone into your mind. You can change where you are by changing what goes into your mind."

Zig Ziglar

Chapter 3
What Are You Thinking?

"You are valuable. It's easy to forget that fact. Therefore, you must see yourself as a champion in order to enter and complete the race."

You are valuable. I need you to know that because many of us probably have never been told that by the person we needed to hear it from the most. That person is *you*. Acknowledgement of self-worth unlocks restrictions of what has passed. No one is "better than you" at defining who you are. You are just as worthy as anyone you know!

Where Are You?

'Where are you?' is a loaded question. Life can lead to confusion. Confusion leads to fear, failure and restriction. Your current circumstances may be real. Yet, what you do to navigate them is where your freedom lies. Confusion can change to clarity when you pay attention. Once clear about what you desire and deserve, you can choose to do the work to live in your destiny. Valuing who you are is so important because without clarity or direction you don't know where you are going. Sometimes it takes an experience to wake us up.

One summer day while driving, I clearly saw the detour signs telling me to take another route. I ignored them. This was my path and I was going to get to my destination. Those signs didn't matter. Caught up in my head I was being stubborn and ended up on a dead end street, literally. Because I knowingly defied the signs, I wasted a lot of time and ended up having to back track to get to my intended location. Once I got back on track, something shifted. I suddenly noticed the hot pavement ahead was a mirage. My perspective began to change.

As I was seeing the mirage with my eyes, I heard God say, *"Your Destiny is Not a Mirage."* I think I chuckled when I heard it. I actually shook my head at myself. I heard the message. It was a sign. I realized I was listening to the message when the mirage began to fade. Signs give direction and clarity, only when we pay attention and follow them. This was surely a sign I would not choose to ignore. This message was about life, my life and future, not just a drive on a hot day.

I had lost my joy. I wanted more but wasn't sure how to have it. The drive was a reflection of my life. This message was an invitation to regain who I could be, should I choose to listen. Making decisions and heading down paths just because I was accustomed to them, not because they were beneficial had been my story. Before that moment, I was confined in confusion and worry, not clear or confident about my life's purpose and path. I was going through the motions.

When I heard Him, I began to listen intently, something I hadn't done well in the past. Looking back, I realize fear of rejection and the unwillingness to further expose my vulnerabilities had made me feel less than appreciative and of no value. But joy creates a heart of gladness when you have inner peace and self-awareness of what is controlling your thoughts and emotions.

Most of the time, we don't know where we want to go which is why we don't recognize the signs when we see them. When we get stuck in routines, old habits or those thoughts which put us on autopilot, we miss some important things along the journey.

Getting to your destiny means removing confusion and anything which is holding you back. It also means looking forward, feeling worthy enough to build a purposeful, joyful future.

"Happy" and "joy" are not one in the same. Happy is emotion-based and doesn't last. Joy is a state of mind and a condition of the heart. Being "full of joy," is possible even when the outside conditions look bleak.

Being Willing

What are you willing to give up? What are you willing to stop avoiding and omitting to get there? After knowing what it is, you can create a plan. If you want to be in a better place, start with where you are and where you want to be, working through the distractions and obstacles. If you don't start the plan, plot the course, and stay on it, nothing will change. Your life will begin to feel like you are living in a mirage and you'll be stuck or think you can't turn around when you have the opportunity.

When life presents a change, like a detour sign along the road, be willing to adjust your direction when necessary because heading in the right direction is far more powerful than going in circles, becoming frustrated or being stuck to routines. *Your Destiny is Not A Mirage.*

Thinking, Saying and Living

"I am valuable." It's a bold and beautiful statement, just like you. When leading with the thought, "I am valuable," we create the space for freedom, leading to joy. Thinking "I am valuable," leads you to look at yourself and life differently. It will keep you going.

Acknowledging where you are in your thinking ensures your mind is clearly focused on the new path you are about to journey. Before getting behind the wheel of self-will, map out where you want to be by establishing your goals, vision and purpose then stick to it! Now get going to new beginnings and new victories! Remain focused on your purpose and keep calm in case of detours.

Chapter 4
What Happened Passed

"It's tempting to give up – and you likely have, repeatedly. Look at you now, pushing beyond the past. It's time to give in to your good. Ready, Set, Escape!"

"Prisoner of war failed at attempted escape."

That's not a newspaper headline, that's the reality for most human beings who want more out of life, but are stuck in a past, which has passed. Most of the time, it's not what's facing us which holds us back, it's what has happened which keeps us gripped. It's not always the circumstances. It's also the fallout from relationships, work and life events which take hold, creating bitterness, confusion and confinement. There's more to life than this.

I can't begin to imagine I know what your life has been – your thoughts, feelings or experiences. I can't begin to imagine the depths of your pain or even the heights of your victories. Yet, you are reading this passage for a reason. This fact tells me you want something more. More you shall have – if you are willing to do something different.

By taking another path you can have a new outcome. Start by making a new decision or new choice. There are alternative routes. If you have discovered that the

---

things you keep doing over and over aren't working, then change your thinking, attitude, mindset, ways of doing it and perhaps your traditions too. As things change in life, and as the world is changing, your thinking has to change if you want to see better, do better and be fulfilled.

No Joy!

"Don't even bother," was my attitude and baseline response to avoid being misunderstood one more time. I would just keep silent though I knew what I was thinking and feeling was important, necessary and could help myself and others. Occasionally, I was even labeled "anti-social," though I wasn't. I felt ineffective because I couldn't express myself in a way others would understand. I don't know if you can relate but, this happened most of my life. I was that way because I was a dreamer and didn't feel people understood me. When I say dreamer, I mean I had meaningful dreams. When I would share my thoughts, often people didn't relate to them. I was afraid. I just learned to withdraw, mainly to feel less judged. I wanted to change because I started noticing my intuition, thoughts and sometimes dreams could have helped people in certain cases had I opened my mouth. I no longer allowed my own self-consciousness to prevent me from contributing to others' lives in meaningful ways.

Once I decided my path could be different, I got committed to speaking up. That decision represented progress. The decision opened the door to my destiny. I began thinking and expressing myself differently, evolving. And so can you.

This is a continuous process. Through awareness, coaching and courage, you will be more confident. People are drawn to confidence. Your self-confidence will lead to new responses and outcomes for you and for others.

Creating Joy

We are FREE to enjoy all God has for us, yet we often discount that fact, allowing "life" to get in the way of purpose. Most of us have at least one thing we do which fulfills us and positively impacts the lives of others. It's that thing we do not only for our benefit but for others too. We know and sense deep within our hearts. It is what we're supposed to be doing and oftentimes others acknowledge our true gift at work too. Can you name it for yourself?

Thinking Healthy

How do you classify yourself? Are you optimistic or pessimistic? Your stance/perspective influences every experience and every choice. Whatever reality we have created for ourselves ends up being what we get. When outsiders look in, they make judgments. What about when you look in? What do you see? Do you like what you see and what you feel? I'm not talking about in the short term, like the view from your window; I'm talking about your day-to-day lifestyle. Do you take time to do healthy things, think healthy thoughts and head down a healthy road or do you wander and take what you can get?

Destiny is not just a destination, a one-time stop where you get a lifetime pass of leisure. It's a daily journey which doesn't change like the weather but can sometimes feel like it does.

Sometimes we find ourselves searching aimlessly for our purpose in life because of the pictures we paint in our mind – leaving us in a state of confusion, doubt, or even depression. You see, you are already living in your destiny. You just have to realize it, embrace it, and enjoy it!

Since we were all created to live a purposeful life, each of us were born with a roadmap to fulfill the lives of one another by using the talents, time, gifts and abilities we have to offer one another. As we live this way, we are creating joy.

Chapter 5
Finding My Freedom

Disappointments and failed expectations no longer rule me.

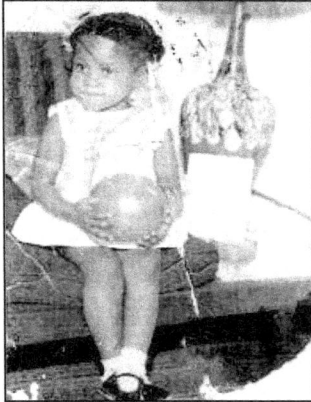

Lavanda Rochelle, Age 5

At times, because I knew I was different than most, I felt ostracized, misunderstood and almost embarrassed because I saw things and understood things that didn't make sense to others. When I would share thoughts, visions or my perspective, oftentimes people would not understand nor appreciate what I was saying. One day, I remember a friend saying, "Whenever I see you bad things seem to be happening with you." This caused me to pause. I didn't see it that way. I saw it as enduring the test I was faced within this season of my life. I no longer allow disappointments and failed expectations to rule me.

The Promised Land, Your Destiny

If you've either read or heard bible stories about Moses and the Israelites, you know their journey from Egypt to the Promised Land took 40 years of wandering the desert. Did you know that the physical trip, based on location and mileage was only an 11 day distance? Yes! To go from Horeb to Kadesh Barnea by the Mount Seir road takes 11 days. They were in the desert, complaining, wandering, acting up, even melting gold and worshipping idols while Moses had meetings with God.

Think about us, me and you today. How old are we? With all of our modern conveniences, proven miracles and available tools and resources, yet, we are still struggling. Re-reading the story and the footnotes found in *The Zondervan and Tynedale House Publisher's Life Application Study Bible*, Deuteronomy, Chapter 1:1-2 was extremely helpful to me because it shed insight on what happened with them and gave me a mirror to view what was happening with me. Here's a summary of what the book says:

"It wasn't the distance that stood between them and the Promised Land. It was the conditions of their hearts. God's purpose went deeper than simply transporting a huge group of people to a new land. He was preparing them to live in obedience to him once they arrived. What good was the Promised Land if the Israelites were just as wicked as the

nations already living there? The journey was a painful but necessary part of their preparation. Through it God taught the Israelites who he was: the living God, the Leader of their nation. He also taught them who they were: people who were fallen, sinful, prone to rebellion and doubt. He gave his people the law to help them understand how to relate to God and to other people. Your spiritual pilgrimage may be lengthy, and you may face pain, discouragement, and difficulties. But remember that God isn't just trying to keep you alive. He wants to prepare you to live in service and devotion to him."

What do you think? Can you see yourself in that explanation? Much like the Israelites whose trip took 40 years, though it should have been a matter of days journeying in the physical, we get impatient, tired, and confused. We lose sight of our purpose and the path that leads us on the journey into our freedom. Sometimes our own negative thinking and lack of faith prevent us from entering into a place that will bring us joy. We find ourselves discouraged and feeling like we are not good enough nor deserving of what lies ahead. Yet when we finally give in, we allow God to guide us into our Promised Land.

Full of Fear

Imagine being lost and locked up deep within, and fearful too. I spent my childhood secretly living in fear. Yes, I said it! I said that word FEAR – false evidence appearing real. I didn't define it that way then. I was just afraid. That's what I knew when I was little. As an adult, I could define fear, had even convinced myself I had overcome it, but really, I had not. Fear existed and stayed with me, a constant companion keeping risk and new possibilities away, blocking my expression from day-to-day.

Growing up I was smart enough to know I was different than kids my age. I don't recall too many days when my family and friends didn't put me on a pedestal. I was smart in school, but deep down I didn't know everything and was ashamed of not knowing. I felt it was expected of me to know more. I found myself trying to live up to the standards of what was spoken in my environment my entire life to ensure I didn't let anyone down. I became afraid of failure. I couldn't find any wiggle room to mess up. I owned the titles I was given such as "professor" or "bookworm." I somehow felt I had to live up to those names, though no one ever said I had to. I was stuck within my own mind, trying to role-play a title. This was the reality of my childhood dramatic play.

Tell yourself repeatedly throughout your day who you are and not what you think you are.

You must verbally tell yourself:

"I am a conqueror",

"I am confident",

"I am never alone".

You fill in the blank now. "I am_____."

Tell yourself until the words are rooted and grounded in your conscious and subconscious because your own voice is not a stranger to you. The more you say it aloud; you will become and see yourself evolve into what you hear yourself think. This in turn will help you endeavor with purpose to complete your God-given destiny.

My Older Friends

I didn't and couldn't act like everyone else. Honestly speaking, I thought kids my age were silly, immature, and simply needed to grow up. Most of the time I enjoyed being alone although I am the sixth of eight children. I loved being off to myself every opportunity I got. My favorite thing to do growing up was hang around older or elderly people. I didn't know then like I know now, that I was attracted to the wisdom they imparted in me. They made sense to me and my age group didn't. In fact, the first church I became a member of when I was a child had an elderly pastor with a predominately elderly congregation. I behaved like them outwardly, but inwardly I was my age, blasting with praise. Yes, blasting with praise and yet longing to live a normal childhood like a child should. I simply couldn't. At least that's what I thought. The Bible says the fear of the LORD is the beginning of Wisdom. So why did I fear? I simply did not have an understanding of why I had "those" dreams.

Not Shy, But Afraid to Dream

I never considered my childhood a normal one because people didn't get me. They didn't understand the nature of who I was and most still don't. When I was at school, my teachers and classmates would tell me I acted like a little old lady. My second oldest brother to this very day calls me "Old Lady." I appeared shy to others but truth is I was scared out of my wits because of the things I would dream.

Chilling Nightmare

What's normal about a child in a dream when she begins to feel the pain her aunt is going through in Wisconsin? Nothing! My heart pained me in my sleep, I shivered, and felt ice cold – stone cold. Within an hour of the dream my mother got a phone call telling her our dearly, beloved great aunt just had a heart attack. My mom took a bus to Wisconsin at daybreak and as she was en route, my aunt passed away. What child's dream is beyond a nightmare? I never wanted to feel like that little girl lost, locked up deep within and fearful.

I tried my best to escape those frightening, unwanted dreams that never made sense, but kept me praying and calling on the name of Jesus, even in my sleep. Often I found myself awakening from them with a racing heart – a pounding and beating in my ear drum and sometimes a body shaking out of fear. Sometimes I would even get up in the middle of the night to sleep in bed with my younger sibling until day break. I didn't tell anyone, but I started sleeping with my Bible open under my pillow on Psalm 23. This Psalm seemed to always calm and bring me peace.

God called me out in my childhood. He began revealing Himself and the call on my life through dreams and even visions. What I saw in these dreams simply terrified me because I was too young to understand and too scared to tell my parents what I was seeing. Although my parents never made it difficult for me to talk to them, I couldn't tell them about these dreams. I kept thinking, "If I utter a word they will think I'm crazy and have me locked up." Back then grown-ups would talk about folks locked up in Alton, Illinois, who had mental disorders. Alton was about thirty minutes away and because of the stories, it seemed like it was next door, waiting to admit me. I knew I wasn't crazy, but I was afraid of them having me locked up too.

Taking Risks Conquers Fear

As with many of us, my childhood filtered into my adulthood. Being fearful filtered that is. It made me overprotective, a mother hen, solemn, timid, and reserved in mannerism. It impacted my relationship with my spouse, my children, and others I became acquainted with. I had to "get it" that *Freedom in Joy* is my right. Experience taught me being fearful was preventing me from fulfilling the God-given destiny on my life, and ultimately my greater/divine purpose. My husband would ask me what I was so afraid of. It took a long time for his frustration to build to tell me about me – by that time, I had asked and was ready to hear it - a good cleansing session, out of love and truth. I appreciate his honesty and constant encouragement.

When I started risking – stepping outside of my natural boundaries – whether it was visiting the neighborhood stores, driving on the highway, establishing new friendships or getting involved in community activities, day by day, I started taking responsibility for my actions. Those steps started to bring joy because each day God was strengthening me.

If you find yourself being overcome and overwhelmed, take a leap of faith and push yourself to be spontaneous without second guessing yourself. Every day learn to explore, embrace, and respond to new changes – new possibilities rather than fear them. Tell yourself: *I can do all things because God will strengthen me for His joy is my strength.*

Turn on your internal GPS to hear and remind yourself daily throughout your journey of the covenant you made to move forward into your destiny and future. Doing so will help keep your thinking on track about where you are and where you are going. Remember you have the electronic roadmap of purpose and goals. The system can only be voice activated by you as a guide that navigates and maintains order in your thoughts and actions along the way. Not activating the system when you know you are lost is choosing to be confined.

Destiny
and
Desire
Life Experiences & Your Purpose

Circumstances can seem bleak, that's the time to get flexible, not stay stuck. Everything which happened to this point prepared you to overcome and to flourish, it's time to make some tough choices. You are tougher than anything which has ever happened to you. Do you know why I know this? Because you are still alive, breathing, and you are reading this sentence. You probably won't want to deal with the hard stuff, but you can and will because you are ready to be free. That's it. Dealing with the distractions will shorten the delays.

You would not have deep desires if your destiny was not for you.

Chapter 6
Living Life

Paying attention to and appropriately responding to the matter at hand is critical to the well-being of everyone, including you.

Mr. and Mrs. Paul Heard

Here We Are, Together

Sometimes we have to be signaled what to do when things are coming at us from every direction. When so many things are happening at once, we can get overwhelmed, overburdened and be overcome. We must be alert concerning the things which cause us to worry. Your destiny is not in the recesses of your mind nor is it in the dimly lit, dark places of your dreams or hurtful, misunderstood past. Though your destiny includes your future, it is right now; present and available. Your Destiny is not a Mirage – it is Real. Welcome to it.

Your Destiny

Your journey has always had a destination; however, it takes time and experience to see it and to live in it. There are difficult moments. Yes, you have experienced heartache and pain. Yes, there are deserted places you might find yourself in, yet you are not stuck even though you may think you are. You are not stuck! At least, you don't have to stay stuck!

Today, in this moment, it's time to move into your destiny before you run out of time. There are thoughts you can think and things you can do to rise above the past and to prepare for the here and right now… the end of suffering, the end of sadness, the end of loss, the end of illness, the end of hiding from who you are, the end of not trusting God, yourself and others, and the end of repressing you, your God-given talents and gifts. Your Destiny is Not a Mirage. It's for real.

Setting the Tone

Being involved is different than being fully committed. You influence your space, and that of others. Harness your energy, aim it in the right direction and rise!

When you walk into a room, do you lift it up or bring it down? It's a good question. If you don't know the answer, you should. Wherever you are, you bring with you energy and possibility. Your perfume, along with volume and tone of voice have an effect on others. When thinking about your freedom and destiny, focus on your activities, to get to where you actually want to be – and stay.

At Home

If you are a parent, you know that school day mornings can sometimes be a challenging experience, especially following a weekend. On the days when I'd have plenty of rest and plenty of time, I would be calm and help my two boys and my husband to be calm as well. They would have an awesome day and so would I.

The opposite is also true. On the days when I was tired, stressed, not rested, felt rushed or worried, I would fuss and hurry them out the door. When that happened, the boys didn't seem to have a great day, especially my older one. I would get a call or note from his school stating that he had acted out in some way. At times he may have talked out in class or even gotten out of his seat. I was even told he would laugh out loud in class and just continue to laugh causing others to do likewise. Those small things soon escalated into inconvenient in-school or after school detentions for my son because I did not set the tone for our family at the start of our day.

I believe subconsciously he was thinking "I didn't have a good day with mom," and thus would act out with female teachers those days, in some way. I think because I was predominantly the disciplinarian and he frequently heard me saying, "Don't do this and don't do that." Now this other person is trying to correct me as well, therefore his attitude reflected "I'm not trying to hear it actions."

This happened mainly when their father would travel for an extended period of time for his job. I was the one to push and steer them in the right direction. After all, they are boys and boys can be tough. Whenever they heard "that voice," they would start shutting down and resisting what I was saying. Yet, I wasn't consistently reinforcing anything I was saying. I didn't follow through on promised consequences for their behavior. They didn't believe anything was going to happen because consequences mostly happened by chance. We repeated this cycle more often than I care to admit.

If I'm not doing something that I'm telling you to do every day, then I'm sending the message that you don't have to do it. When I was stressed and not paying attention to the mere fact of what I was doing or saying like rushing, fussing, or worrying, I set the tone for that day and showed them it was okay for them to act up like me. What about you?

Being Calm and Consistent

When you feel stressed or worried, stop what you are doing. Take a deep breath or remove yourself from what's pulling on you at the moment. See if what you are drawn into is really worth the trouble. Pray, yell to the top of your lungs, or do whatever that thing is that relaxes you. Read a book, go jogging, take a walk or get in the shower. Do something that's not going to cause you to stress or worry later. Spending time on what you desire in life instead of what you are trying to avoid frees your thoughts, emotions and energy.

Freedom?

Releasing the past, embracing the now, creating the future, and knowing where you intend to be, is where Freedom is found. My Destiny is Not a Mirage! Thank God I know that now.

Chapter 7
Stepping Into the Vision

"Write down the revelation and make it plain on tablets so that a herald may run with it. For the revelation awaits an appointed time; it speaks of the end and will not prove false Though it linger, wait for it; it will certainly come and will not delay."

Habakkuk 2:2-3

Your thoughts are potent. Potent means powerful. Power denotes ability. You have the ability to change your thought process by gaining a different view. The way you change your perceptions and mindset is by allowing yourself to be flexible and open-minded to receive fresh thoughts, new opportunities and new possibilities. You must trust yourself and believe you are capable of shifting to a new position. Taking the risks is the first milestone to succeeding. This means having the faith to move outside your common space of what is comfortable and habitual for you and transitioning to embrace what is live and active inside of you …your destiny. It has been said, "The sky is the limit to what I can have."

Challenge yourself to see beyond the sky. See yourself enrolled in college and graduating with honors, CEO of your own company, losing your desired weight, catching the biggest fish in the lake, taking that much needed walk or whatever it is.

You have the power and ability to achieve and exceed your potential when you focus on reaching that goal. Focus requires concentration. Concentrating on fulfillment means filtering your thoughts and heart (generating courage) with the fuel to reach your destination.

What do you see yourself doing?

What is it that you have always desired to do?

You must know what you were created on this earth to do and see yourself as the person doing it.

If you are struggling with answering either of those questions, I suggest you take a moment to pause your reading, after completing this chapter, long enough to write down your vision, natural abilities, purpose and goals in life to keep your thoughts and attention focused in the direction you are headed.

Writing a plan will help you to:

1. Read what you have written

2. Keep your commitment to yourself

3. Maneuver around the obstacles and road blocks you encounter along the way

4. Keep you from getting stuck in a rut.

Take time now to ask yourself the following questions then write down your response:

1. *Where do I see myself going?*

2. *What is my purpose in life? How can I equip myself to fulfill it?*

3. *What are my short term and long term goals?*

4. *How am I going to reach my goals?*

5. *When do I plan to reach my goals?*

6. *What is it that I do that positively impact others and fulfills me?*

Chapter 8
Laboring

You will eat the fruit of your labor; blessings and prosperity will be yours.

Psalm 128:1-3

When you find yourself struggling, you will find out what you're really made of.   How you handle yourself in those moments will take you off course, keep you at bay, or help you thrive in your destiny. Think about your home life and your work life.   Are there certain situations or relationships which are preventing you from Freedom in Joy?   Sometimes you will find yourself laboring with your single life, your marriage, raising a stubborn child, laboring with a difficult boss or co-worker, or laboring with everyday decisions and circumstances with built in challenges. That's life. Losing some struggles can free your life, resulting in rebirth.

What Are You Trying To Control?

Choose what you're going to do to overcome them and do it out of love and self-control rather than manipulation and control.

You, like me, may need to give up trying to control people and situations. I found myself struggling with many things such as trust, fear, and over-nurturing any and everything because I felt like I had to protect everyone. I felt like I had to be the one to save the world. Once I noticed what was happening and its effects, I decided to stop. It took practice and consistent effort. I was willing to release those thoughts and behavior patterns in order to gain guidance, healing, and ultimately freedom in God. Thank God I am consciously aware of my need to control situations so I stop hurting and pushing anxiety off on others. It's important to be able to release whatever we are battling with or holding on to.

Loosening Control

Bottom line, you must consciously make yourself aware of what is causing a tug of war in your thoughts and actions. Then focus your attention to what is in front of you so you don't continue to miss out on what lies ahead of you. You must purposefully and intently turn your attention back to what's being said or the issue at hand so you will know what to do when you find yourself wandering back down that path of "must be in control". Refocusing yourself will help you to become aware of what you are thinking, saying and doing and then cause you to respond appropriately, which is critical to the well-being of everyone, including you.

Bringing my children into this world was like laboring with life itself. It took a lot from me and also brought joy greater than I can express. Think about times when you were determined to get to a place, complete a project or bring something or someone to life, and you did it! Was it easy? Probably not. Yet, you were persistent and hung in there until you made it to your expected end.   Failure was never an option.   How do I know? You didn't give up or give in.   Whatever you take from the experience and however you feel about the end result will influence your attitude and perspective. Learning to take lessons, overcome challenges and embracing the outcome is key to creating patterns of success.

When we are birthing something new, truth is, it is painful and exhausting. It is difficult to take those slow, deep breaths when the pain level is at its peak. We feel it because of the sacrificing, giving, and yielding of ourselves to the birth. If we allow God's voice to calm us and to relax us, even when we feel the urge to blow up, we will birth our bundle of joy – peace, deliverance, hope, healing, success, abundance, family, friends, promotion, and joy.

Labor and Childbirth

Childbirth labor, like life, takes something out of you. You will sweat and you will feel what you are going through. Nevertheless when God himself says to push, you push. And when he says, "take a rest," that means stop what you are doing and rest. While you rest, God is taking over, coaching you through this painful situation.

Both of my pregnancies were high-risk. I went into preterm labor with my first son and was in an auto accident during the pregnancy with my second son. When I was going through my high-risks prenatal experiences, I wanted to act out or behave insensibly, but ultimately chose not to because I was able to refocus on the issue at hand - a full term delivery without further complications. This is what you must do to prevent further delay in your life's journey. You have to be willing to pay attention to the issue at hand and begin to do what is right and healthy for you to reach a joyful ending… your destiny.

My journey into the experience of motherhood was not easy. During both of my pregnancies I questioned – with good reason, if I would live to see my children, let alone, if they would live to see me. My skin tone was the color of dark chocolate and my vocals were deeper than any man I know on any given day. I couldn't even stand to look in the mirror because I didn't like all the changes I saw in me.

Every day we awaken to our reality and encounter the changes that come with it. We sometimes can't find our joy in that moment and fail to realize the joy still resides within us. It's just that when we are not in that place of freedom to receive it, we don't realize it's ours anymore. It is then you must refocus yourself and choose what's good rather than harmful for you. The fact of the matter is, "I know I'm in this, but how do I get out?"

As I share my prenatal experience with my firstborn son, Joshua, I want you to examine your own experiences, thoughts, and motives, especially during difficult times. Think about your attitude, your determination and your choosing. Are you proud of your choices? You should be. If not, do something about it. Though your experience may be different from mine, it's for real. In the midst of your hurt and pain, you must still choose to come out victoriously. You must choose to rise above your thinking as I had to. Choosing, in this context means thinking differently, having the right motive, believing in yourself, and finding the hope within yourself so you can move forward into something new, better, and even greater.

At the beginning of my sixth month of pregnancy I was leaving church and began to feel an excruciatingly sharp pain in my lower back. The next day, Monday morning after arriving at work, I felt the same sharp pain again. It felt like it was in my head too. This led to an emergency office visit with the Obstetrician. My OB/GYN said my cervix had effaced 80%, meaning 20% more thinning and I would be in active labor. It was too early.

His nurse flat out said, "This means if the baby comes now, you will have a stillborn birth." I wanted to shake or hit her for being so negative. Though nervous and scared, I did my best to ignore those words. I just couldn't come to grips with the fact that it took me a whole year to get pregnant and now it could possibly end. I was put on complete bed rest until his birth. Thank God my OB/GYN knew Him, God that is, though his nurse didn't seem to. My doctor gave me hope in a seemingly hopeless situation that *I might not lose the baby*.

"I contacted your insurance and told them you require home monitoring and that this baby can be either a million dollar baby or a $15,000 baby. It's your choice!" Said our doctor to the insurance company, who did not want to foot the bill for saving the baby. We were shocked and then delighted as the doctor explained that the insurance company agreed to have a company called Tokos monitor me at home after having several ER visits.

Tokos provided similar services one would receive at a hospital stay. My medication was delivered to my front door. The nurses from the local hospital came out to my home to perform all normal office visit procedures as well as to teach me how to inject and change my IV line, which was attached to a palm sized device that ran medicine in my body 24 hours a day. I changed the line every four days. I had a home uterine activity monitor for them to see the number of contractions I was having per hour each day. Emergency numbers were stored in it to call for help at the touch of a button. If I'd have too many contractions while asleep or awake, they'd call me to have me administer more doses of medicine in my body to prevent preterm birth. It was not easy or simple, yet I reminded myself to be grateful.

Being Reflectively Thankful

I was so thankful I had more than enough prayers and support to get me through. Think about all the times when you least expected it, someone gave you money to buy groceries when your cupboard was empty or a check came in mail when you had a final notice on your gas or electric bill or perhaps when your gas tank was on empty. Provisions were made when you were at the brink of giving up. These moments encourage, uplift, inspire, and remind us to never lose hope. God knew I could not afford the high medical expense which comes with hospitalization. I was grateful for both the tangible and intangible blessings I had received. Joshua was born healthy, happy and at full term!

When you're having an unpleasant day and someone walks up to you and simply smiles, says good morning, asks how are you or may I help you, you soon forget what has been weighing on you so heavily. You can also be that smile for others. When your attitude is focused forward, it's much easier to share good along the way.

A Sibling's Intuition

When I was pregnant the second time, with Joseph, Joshua crawled up in my lap one day and while pointing to my stomach said "Look Mommie! My sister Joseph." I laughed just like you're probably doing right now. I kept telling him "Mommie doesn't have a baby in her tummy." Later Joshua became ill and was taken to the ER. When it was time for his x-rays, the technician wanted to know if I were pregnant before allowing me to enter the x-ray room. I said, "No, but he keeps telling me I am." The technician recommended I see my doctor for a pregnancy test and not enter the x-ray room. I took the advice only to learn Joshua was right. I was indeed pregnant. How did he know before I did? God knows.

Why Intuition Matters

The Heard Family

Perhaps you are wondering why intuition matters. It matters because our intuition tells us what we should do or refrain from doing in a given situation, though we often times find ourselves back in that old habit of ignoring the road signs ahead of us. We find ourselves yielding to our set ways of taking the popular path that leads to wandering in a maze of worry, confusion, doubt, loneliness and depression instead of the path that leads directly to our destiny.

We know from past experiences the destruction it will bring us yet we find ourselves giving in to our reckless thoughts again. You must choose to alter your mindset when you know in your heart a detour is necessary for you to continue your journey. When we listen to our intuition, we enter new realms of possibility. When you align your intuition with your vision and are intentional, you excel.

Chapter 9
When You Need Hope

*But without faith it is impossible to please him: for he that
cometh to God must believe that he is, and that he is a
rewarder of them that diligently seek him.*

Hebrews 11:6

My mother taught me that faith is priceless. It is more than any money can ever buy. When I was elementary school age, I asked my mom for money to buy something; this was before I had started receiving allowance. When my mom told me she didn't have any money, I became angry with her because I had never approached her for money before. My mom became silent, walked away, and returned with the monthly bills. I sat down at the kitchen table and added them all up only to get a rude awakening, she had more bills than money.

For the first time in my life, other than when my great aunt became deathly ill, I saw tears roll down my mother's cheek. I felt worse than bad for asking her for money. To this very day, I don't believe those tears were shed out of lack, but because she reflected on how God had provided and was still providing for her and her eight children in spite of our low family income. I believe she knew as long as she kept her faith, we would never be without the things we needed in our life's journey. From that day forward my mom became my hero - Woman of Faith. God bless my mother for the faith she had back then and still has today.

I also learned that no matter what circumstance I find myself in, I will never be without if I don't lose my faith, hope, and trust in God. Even though my mom didn't have enough money, our needs were met - we had a roof over our head, food to eat, clothes on our back, and good health. My siblings and I never even realized the lack because we embraced what we had and was grateful and thankful for that.

Gratitude leads to destiny. Although you may not have everything you want or desire right now, if you just focus or turn your attention towards the many blessings you already have, you will begin to enjoy an abundant life. What do you already have plenty of? Abundance is yours to have and to share with others not to hold. No matter what your struggles are this present day, I pray that you begin to appreciate what you do have and never lose hope in what is yet to come! I pray the hope inside you causes you to smile a smile big enough to encourage someone else to never stop believing either.

I want to share a poem with you written to my mother, Alberta Holman, for Mother's Day, in appreciation of her teaching me by example how to be a strong woman of faith through her life and everyday living from my childhood to adulthood.

We tend to lose faith in God when we are going through hardships and things aren't going our way. If you find yourself laboring in work, in your finances, self-esteem, in a relationship or in some other area of your life that's robbing you of your joy, this is a poem you may read, think about or perhaps consider and see yourself in joy, see yourself courageous, see yourself empowered, see yourself claiming abundance in that moment. You might have to go back over and over again to read it until you see the possible. It's okay. Going back to read it lets me know that you are making a choice. Now you have something to signal you when you go back into your old way of thinking, being or doing things.

Here's a reminder for you, a poem I wrote a while back.

Woman of Faith

One day you asked me what's my favorite scripture of faith.
I said "I don't have a particular one"
It's whatever God gives me to teach and speak
Cause I'm a Woman of Faith
Yes, when I stand, whatever God gives me
I just tell it until they heed it
cause I'm a Woman of Faith.

You see, I've got testimony upon testimony
of how good God's been to me.
To live and see my children good and grown
and even my grandchildren's children
cause I'm a Woman of Faith.

I know what it's like to have gifted hands
to sew my children's clothes, to wash them, and
pin them to a clothesline to dry on a hot summer's day
cause I'm a Woman of Faith.

I know what it's like to have seasons of more bills than money.
To be burned out of what I called 'home' on an ice cold winter's day
with children scattered here and there
yet know, that I know Jehovah Jireh, my provider
cause I'm a Woman of Faith.

I know the power of prayer over a hot home cooked meal
stretched not only to feed my own but a
neighborhood of family and friends
cause I'm a Woman of Faith.

So, if you ask me again what's my favorite scripture of faith
and I just had to choose one
I'd say "Faith the size of a mustard seed"
cause I'm a Woman of Faith.

Lavanda Rochelle Heard   49

Chapter 10
When You Need Restoration

The Lord is my shepherd, I lack nothing. He makes me lie down in green pastures, he leads me beside quiet waters, he refreshes my soul.

Psalm 23:1-3 NIV

Be Courageous Through Fear

When I was a teenager a minister, a man of God, whom I trusted, kissed me against my will. This incident shattered my concept and expectation of ministers, grown men and the church. I felt violated, ashamed, embarrassed and angry. He had no right to do that to me. I experienced fall out as a result of the situation because I took a stand and reported the incident. He did not appreciate the fact that I revealed what he had done. I was ostracized and treated as if I had done something inappropriate to him, not the other way around. His behavior impacted the way I saw myself, as well as the way I saw men. Because I felt violated so early in life, I occasionally kept my guards up with my husband until I permitted myself to release and let it go.

Things will happen in life and sometimes we don't have control. However, learning from situations and moving forward through forgiveness is important to us regardless if the offender learns a lesson or not. Forgiveness releases you from what has passed, even though you still remember, and gives you courage to stand above the very thing you once feared, denied, and perhaps despised. You must forgive from the heart not out of your emotions. Forgiving someone from the depths of your heart will allow you to move on, but forgiving out of emotions will permit you to revisit your experience, delaying your healing.

A couple of years later I had a similar experience at another church. I had to look at myself and ask why this was happening to me. Something about my demeanor must have had them feel I wouldn't stand up for myself. I realized it was because I was reserved, shy, and quiet. As a result of me rejecting him, he retaliated to cover up his own transgressions. I later discovered he was involved with one of my peers. He never approached me again because I stood up for myself with great strength and boldness. I had courage to hold my head up high, look my offender straight in the eyes, and move through, forgiving him (not-verbally, but internally). I also prayed for this minister – he was the adult, after all, and what he had done was not acceptable.

Seek Healing

In May 2012, I had surgery on my shoulder to regain the rotation of my left arm due to a tear. I spent six weeks in an arm sling and six months in physical therapy. I was on very heavy pain medication day in-night out.

I needed it to end. Afraid of becoming addicted to the strong pain medication I had become accustomed to taking, I cried out to God. I spent the entire weekend fasting and praying. Fasting for me was remaining locked up in my bedroom the entire weekend with no phone calls or television, and meeting my sons' needs not wants. I remained in God's presence praying, talking to Him, and reading my Bible. I told God I was tired of all the pain and pain medication that was now nurturing me, and simply needed Him to heal me.

That night, I fell asleep and saw Matthew 11:28 in a dream. When I awakened from my dream, I sat up in bed and grabbed for my Bible that was lying on my nightstand. It read "Come to me, all you who labor and are heavy laden, and I will give you rest." After I read the scripture I realized the pain had eased and I never took any heavy pain medication again. I know healing is possible when we believe in Him.

I desire to be helpful because I have a heart and love for people. I want to see you make it in life and be happy and joyful rather than sad because of things that have caused you hurt and pain. Whatever you are going through won't last forever if you are willing to stop dozing off or sleeping through your pain. Wake up! Sit up! Now EAT the meal placed before you to help regain your physical, mental, spiritual and emotional strength.

We can feel strengthened when we are talking to and in the presence of others, but every single one of us at some point and time in our lives feel down and alone, all of us go through that. It just might not happen as frequently for some as others. But when it does happen, we just need to remind ourselves to get back on track and move forward. The reality is that you may be happy in one area of your life, not be happy in another or may not exactly be satisfied with another area as you'd like, but you're thinking about how it can be better to live a life of freedom.

When you find yourself sick of not moving forward in a certain area of your life though you know you should be, read this poem "Thinking of You," I wrote for my mom number two, Amelia Ballinger. I became acquainted with her in Sunday School at our church and was able to visit during her hospital stay a few years ago. Personalize it with your name so it speaks directly to you. Let it speak to you before the dawn of day, upon awakening, before resting at night, throughout the day or whatever hour you need it most. Wake up, arise, and feast on the beauty of a brand new day ready to give you back your health and strength. Tell yourself or someone today, "I'm Thinking of You."

Thinking of You

I'm thinking of you today.
Yes, you with your head turned looking the other way
as if I were talking to someone else other than you.

When I arose this morning,
after saying my prayers,
thoughts of you rested on my mind.

I kept thinking about how beautiful you are inside/out.
Your smile and laughter that's contagious to anyone you meet.
I even solemnly thought about the things
you've been going through lately -
the battle of the mind, body, and soul.

And so I hurl this thought to you
that's resting deep within my inner being --
set your thoughts on things on high
then your mind will be free to dance a sweet melody.

Chapter 11
Passing Through

Storms come to add, then they pass.

Sometimes we will never know why a particular storm came to pass. Acknowledge it happened, take any deposits/lessons and move on. Circumstances and situations in your life are like mirages. They make you think you are at your limit. They cause you to think you can't take cover when you see the storm coming right at you or move to high places when you see the flood waters are knee deep. We believe they are permanent and eternal rather than temporary and momentary. Each of us face situations in our lives that others have already faced and have overcome at one point in time. When you feel like you've been pushed beyond your limit, hang in there. There's someone you can depend on to help you get through it. You have the most powerful force available to you at all times.

Weathering the Storm with Faith

Being surrounded in glass in the midst of a tornado can get you killed. When whirlwinds are coming at you in life, you must take cover! When we're in tornado season, I find myself calling my family together and then running down into our basement to safety. The strong, boisterous winds will inevitably come to shatter the fragile areas of your life, but not destroy you if you pay attention to the storm alerts of your heart and listen for sirens of intuition which warns you to take cover for your own good. There's always a safe place to stand while allowing the storm to pass over. If we just remember to remain calm, stop worrying, hold on to our hope, and not go at it alone the scenery will change. We'll be able to walk through the whirlwinds of life as though they were a cool summer breeze on our cheek. We will find strength to press our way through the conflicts until things can be right in our lives. It may be difficult to accept certain things and embrace the changes, but we will be okay.

I noticed that when things go wrong in my life, I dig deep within my mind to analyze what possibly went wrong and try to find a solution. Sometimes things will happen in life that doesn't make sense at all and we will never have an answer to the "why." It could be obstacles trying to keep the blinders on, however, don't focus on them. Just take that moment to retreat or get into your own space away from the outside noise, chatter, and danger so you can regroup. That is, be still and allow yourself to weather the storm.

Your destiny is not a mirage. My destiny is not a mirage. We are already in it. We must embrace it. I reflect on two dreams; the storm and the flood. I was shown the dry spots in the flood to navigate me out of a situation I feared would drown me. I was given firmly planted feet to stabilize me and then help me escape the chaos surrounding me in the midst of the storm. You must stand firm in the hope God has placed within you when life is just too fearful and overbearing.

Walking in Freedom

One thing I do know is God kept allowing me to feel his presence and protection in spite of my storms. He kept showing me He was my refuge and there was shelter in the midst of each storm. I always had a way out of some of the coldest and darkest places that appeared in my mind like the pit of hell. During those moments I felt alone and scared, God was there to rescue me when I began to pray and call on his name. I believe God himself was teaching me the power of prayer, trusting, believing, and boldly standing in adversity.

Whenever you find yourself afraid to face another day of what you call "hell," know that God has given you power, strength and might to stand boldly; to overcome any negative thoughts you may be battling with in your mind. You have the power to mentally escape anything that oppress and distress you. Escape does not equal hide. It means standing up and facing the different things you are going through head-on. If you haven't already heard or don't know, let me tell you this: You were born a conqueror!

Keep moving, keep standing and keep remembering. Your Destiny is Not A Mirage. Your joy is inside you.

Chapter 12
Strength Through Change

"I was just going through the motions because my heart wasn't in it."

When it comes to mindset, it's not easy to change. Even small adjustments can be difficult. My friend asked me to drive to St. Louis, Missouri, which would require me to cross the Mississippi River and drive about 20 miles from my house, into another state. I immediately got nervous when she asked me. My stomach began to knot up. I felt my heart racing and began to think to myself *I can't drive to St. Louis. I'm afraid of getting lost.* I found myself sitting at my home, in a panic, not wanting to drive away from my neighborhood, let alone the state of Illinois. I was mentally and emotionally resisting being taken out of my comfort zone, after all it was home. The nerve of me to get in a panic and tell myself I'm lost before I had even attempted the drive.

An even bigger transition was when my husband was offered a job in the Middle East and accepted it. This decision meant our family would be moving out of the country. Being in unity as a couple was a crucial factor in making this decision. Though hesitant, I was willing to go because our family would be together, except our older son who was joining the U.S. Marines at the time.

However, when my spouse thought it was a good idea to sell our house, I didn't want to sell it. I must tell the truth. I honestly wasn't ready for another change. Our family and friends were primarily in Illinois and we were leaving the country. Leaving the country as a family was one thing but selling our house, not having a place of our own waiting for us upon our return was too much to handle. I was fearful, anxious, angry and felt lost. Because I love and respect my husband I came into agreement with him. We listed the house.

In preparation for the move, we teamed up to complete all necessary paperwork. Unfortunately, his assignment overseas required his leaving the country before all the manual labor was complete, leaving me to separate out three shipments of household goods. When I started the process, I was just going through the motions because my heart wasn't in it. He did not leave me hanging. We communicated regularly and he did what he could through phone support but it wasn't the same as him being there. It was overwhelming.

Leaving It All Behind for the Middle East

I was feeling loss and thus was reluctant to accept the change at first. I could not visibly see I was granted an opportunity to journey far beyond what I had grown accustomed to. This would be a life changing experience. Having to shift to something new and different is difficult for many of us. It doesn't feel good not knowing what to expect or what you're really getting yourself into until you get there and experience the newness. It requires leaving your past behind, being flexible, giving up control of things you cannot change, and moving forward to doing something new that you've never done before.

Getting Past the Language Barriers

I had an opportunity while living in the Middle East to take a position as a receptionist. Though I have been a business owner, I obtained this position of receptionist at the DoDDS School (The Department of Defense Dependent School). I was told that as a civilian, I probably would not get a job. My husband told me to go over and volunteer and I did. I became a volunteer and as a result of my good service, they asked me to apply for a paying position. It was God's Destiny for that season.

In the beginning, I really didn't desire it and felt nervous because I wasn't sure I would get through the language barrier; however, I grew to love it because I was able to share. This position did not allow me to be in the classroom where I really wanted to be; it took the comfort of being in the classroom from me. I had to be out in the open and communicate with people on another level that I wasn't used to. It was easy to hide in that small space and now I was in the open. I've never been a confrontational person nor wanted to tell grownups what to do. In this position, I was directing people and it was at another level altogether. I had the opportunity to meet and serve people from 13 different countries. I really enjoyed that work.

Choosing to Have a Great Attitude

A receptionist receives people, helps people, gives guidance and is a liaison who sets the tone and the pace for the physical space in an environment. When the person is mean and nasty, it creates bitterness and turns people off. Have you ever called a place of business and was rubbed the wrong way by the person who answered the phone? It happens quite a lot in today's society. The same is true for people who greet others when you come in the door. When entering a restaurant and the people greet you with a smile while saying hello, it can be jolting and unexpected, yet pleasant. Have you had that happen?

One day a parent asked, "Don't you ever get upset about anything?" I answered, "Absolutely, but I just choose not to bring my personal issues to the workplace. This affects the flow and dispositions of not only the visitors but everyone I was hired to work with, support, and interact with daily." He smiled at that answer. I was the first person whom they saw when they walked through that door. I knew they needed to see calmness in me because I set the tone for not only the people, but also for the day.

I wanted to reassure everyone this was a safe place for them. Because we were living in a danger zone – it was important for them to know that we were each other's extended family. You can live a more purposeful life by choosing to have the right attitude and by responding in a more positive way towards others to be the difference and make a difference in their lives for the better. The way you respond to others or handle others tells a lot about your personality, character and destiny. That is, how you perceive yourself and where you see yourself going in life.

As parents we sometimes get upset with our children because they reflect us and we don't like what we see. I made a point that day to speak encouragement and not act out because I know the way you send a person out is the way the rest of their day will go. We set the atmosphere wherever we are. If I am afraid to speak up then you won't receive what God has given me to give to you.

During my first week working as a receptionist, I had to face my Goliath, who wanted to bypass visitor's check-in and walk straight to his child's classroom. We had conversation that eventually led to showing him written school policies. From this experience, he thanked me for how I handled the situation because I protected his child and every student that day. I had earned his respect. I stood up to him that day. I spoke firmly because there is an order to everything and if we don't maintain it, our lives become chaotic.

So, when you are tempted to undermine your destiny by canceling an appointment, not making a phone call, hiding when you are supposed to shine or letting days pass you by because you are afraid you won't be heard or understood, stop acting up!!! It's so real and I have to remind myself of that every single day. Freedom in Joy is about being in the very moment and facing whatever is before you. Greeting it, receiving it, and setting standards for yourself and others about how you will handle things for the good of all involved.

True safety requires calmness, trust and confidence that the words will come in the moment because your foundation is strong.

Moses and Me?

With the excuses, I had claimed that I was Moses. I had been living in a mirage like I immediately thought "I can't speak eloquently." "They won't listen." "I don't know how to say it." "They won't understand." And not only did I think those things, I spoke those things into existence over my life. I was real comfortable thinking I was Moses. You know, he could see how people were acting up and acting out. Truth be told, I would come down from my mountain and throw those tablets! I did it and wanted to fight. Folks in the church acting up. Folks in the streets acting up. Folks in their homes acting up. I did not like it and could not stand it. I was thoroughly angry when people didn't love God the way I love God. I just wanted them to follow God and obey.

I thought, you use God's name, but yet you don't give him the time of day. You quote scripture, but you don't follow what it says. When you get in trouble, the first name you call is God. Yet, when you get a raise, a promotion, a new car or things are going well, you don't even think about Him. That's wrong and I wanted to correct that in the worst way. I do know how to act up too, you know. I had figured out how to do it my way. God Corrected Me.

See, I was able to be that calm, cool storm. People didn't even know how mad I was and how deeply I was judging others disobedience. They don't follow. They do what they want to do. Did I have the right to point my finger at anyone? Of course not! I did what I wanted to do too.

Acting Up

I was driving down the road I normally take to get to my house. This particular day, I was in a crunch and a rush. I had committed to doing something on short notice so, I found a clever way to act up. The first sign, upon approaching the intersection that would have led me directly to where I intended to go said, "Road Closed: Detour." I read the sign and then chose to keep going, to turn onto another street instead of simply following the detour sign. As I drove down that street, it said, "Detour Here." I ignored that sign and kept driving. I kept driving until the street ran out. At the end of that street, the sign said, "Dead End." I had to turn around.

Why did I do any of that? I thought it was just going to lead me to where I needed to go. I didn't want to veer off again, and I was comfortable with my regular path. This detour was an unwelcome distraction and simply a waste of my time, or so I thought. Following this path to the dead end took me places I really didn't want to go. Sitting here today, I realize that much like that drive, I have ignored many signs in my lifetime and instead of following the clear and concise directions that had been placed in front of me for my benefit, I chose not to see.

I take a deep breath, shake my head and smile in this very moment. It's so much larger than a road sign. *We should make plans—counting on God to direct us. Proverbs 16:9*

You see, we can take the straight and narrow or the broad road to hearing, receiving and acting upon the word. The journey we take, scenic or non-scenic route, will still lead us back on the road to God's purpose for our life.

Detours Lead to Destiny

So, it was time to change my approach and live what I was purposed and destined to do. I was projecting my own sense of personal power and desires on others without realizing that I was doing my own thing just like they were. It was my way, not God's way. Umm umm. I'm shaking my head at myself.

Moses didn't make it to the promised land. He led the way, but could not go into it. When we keep asking God for things but we don't listen and follow what he's saying, destiny remains a mirage. When I stop trying to be in control, stop trying to tell others through frustration and acting out, it becomes a reality. I have thought, "Why aren't you serving the way I'm serving and then I have to stop myself!" what have I been doing? Hiding and not speaking up.

Too many of you have been waiting to get comfortable in your destiny and yet, you didn't feel worthy because you felt you were lacking something. Perhaps your pain, your pride, your ego or your past had said, "Shut up, you're crazy" or Shut up, you talk too much" or "Shut up you've been too detached from yourself"? Well, that's not The Truth, though it may be your truth.

Today, I stand with my charge, led by God and given words that He used Paul to speak. It's not just a new day or a new season, it is time – the appointed time to be Bold in the Lord, not in anger or in wrath. Not in breaking things emotionally, fussing, complaining or worrying, but in love, light, in voice and in heart. Honor is yours. Love is yours. Forgiveness is yours and Holiness is yours.

Freedom in Joy is not simply a destination, it is the realization that the Truth lies within you, and when you step into your own destiny, you bring others with you. I love God, I love me, and through loving God, I am able, willing and ready to love you. Your Destiny is not a mirage. So, instead of taking 40 years on a journey, like Moses and the Israelites, I suggest spending 40 days focused on loving ourselves to rest in Joy.

Getting Rid of Excuses

I have recently become aware that I have undermined the power and authority God has given me by declaring failure before I even tried, without being consciously aware of it. One day a friend asked me to type a couple of sentences and the first thing that came out of my mouth was, "I don't type as fast as you do." When my friend pointed that out to me, I was ashamed. Not at her for telling me, but of myself for saying it because I had been doing that for too long. Even when I gave the computer back I said, "Make sure I didn't erase anything on accident." I'm telling you, it's the life I give my thoughts and words that make or break me. I started talking differently, and less frequently. It helps.

Sometimes we have to be signaled what to do when things are coming at us from every direction and be alert concerning the things that causes us to worry. During my "Mirage Day Experience," I noticed the signal lights, among other things, as I was driving. I came up with a formula for changing that habit. This will help you too.

1. God firmly calling my name 'Rochelle' got my attention right away and brought my thoughts/words of negativity to a halt (red light).

2. Being cautioned about what I speak into existence over my life, (yellow light), gave me a chance to change my thoughts and choose words which will bring about true and desired results for me versus what is contradictory to what God said. In other words, not falling for the mirage.

God knows what it will take for me and you to rise. He brings people and situations to stabilize us, at the times when we need them most. He knows the insides and out.

He waits for the appointed time for us to come to ourselves, so we can function through Him versus through our own strength and might.

3. Rest yourself. (Green light). Thanks for signaling me to speak god's promises over my life means that I approach my thoughts and feelings by keeping calm, cool and collected with peace in mind.

Allowing God's light, love and guidance to give me direction and comfort. Comfort does not come without change nor without cost. Comfort does not remain stuck. It comes with a cost. Comfort is God's spirit forever transforming us while, resting in His spirit means I move, I jump, I breathe, I speak, I act and I don't question even when it results in a learning lesson.

Chapter 13
Marriage and Family Practices

Death and life are in the power of the tongue, and those who love it will eat its fruit.

Proverbs 18:21

Connections lift you or bring you down. The person you marry influences just about every choice you make. If you are already attached to your spouse, then you get to make the best from what you have. If you are single, consider what you value most and be sure the person you marry is agreeable to you, your purpose and plan.

Before and after getting married, my parents, grandmother and mother-in-law gave me a few rules to live by to create a long-lasting marriage. I half-way listened and sometimes applied, initially. With time, experience and deeper challenges I began to commit to living to them – in practice.

Golden Practices for Marriage

1. Before and after marriage: Keep God first, remember to pray, and have faith.

2. Make sure you respect him. Two people can't wear the same pants.

3. If he gets sick, not meaning a cold, with a serious illness stick by his side.

4. If your husband likes to go fishing and you don't, GO! Keep Jane off his hook.

5. If you are really deep in the ditch and need advice, then come to mom and dad.

6. Don't hold back intimacy with him just because you are mad at him.

7. Don't try to live like the Jones'. Don't try to be like others.

8. Save and invest your money in IRAs and stocks. Read *Common Sense* investments book.

9. What goes on between you and your husband is the two of your business. When you're done being mad at him, we will still be mad at him. So, work it out.

10. If your husband asks " what's wrong", don't say to him 'nothing' if it's something. Tell him what's wrong.

Women and Men, We Are Different

Amos 3:3 in the bible says, "Do two walk together unless they have agreed to do so?" Do not expect men to see things, experience things or feel the same way you do. Do ask for guidance, direction and a listening, loving ear along with a patient and tame tongue when it comes to communication and harmony. What you think, feel and speak can kill or give life.

Your inner most thoughts, what's going on with, and what you think of you is your truth. If you don't love you, you will not truly love someone else. Keep aware of your heart condition. Your behavior is creating or disintegrating. Should you desire harmony, work through things to get there. Hold on to your love and share it with your spouse!

Married Already? Continue the Chase

When you were dating, you chased hard after each other by spending time communicating and doing things together. Marriage requires the same, and then some. Keep chasing in your relationship with your spouse, in the natural and in the spiritual. Walk with God, never stop chasing after God. Spending time together building an intimate relationship with each other is the same thing God wants from you. Relationship and fellowship go hand in hand so you draw closer to one another.

He's going in one direction and you are going in another. That does not work. The Bible says to seek God first. What does that really mean? When it comes to who you spend your time, temple and life with, it's important not to trust in your own understanding. We as humans can create images which are simply mirages about our mates. However, who you marry will surely affect your destiny.

Not Married? Choose Wisely

Choosing for yourself is very dangerous. I caution you not to use your own judgment regarding your spouse. Though it is important to have values and standards and an idea of what you want and you don't want, it's important that you allow God to lead the process. Being ready for your spouse takes preparation and the Lord is the ultimate Way Maker and Strategic Planner.

You can choose in the will or out of the will of God. When you know what the Word says about a husband and a wife, you must make choices. These choices come from trusting God; let me share one of many important Bible verses:

Trust in the Lord with all your heart and lean not on your own understanding; in ALL your ways acknowledge him, and he will make your paths straight.   Proverbs 3:5-6

You must choose based on the Word, not based on the world or based on your timing. God says to trust him so take it seriously. When you have reached a certain point in your life where you have established a relationship with God, do not drag a person who does not share your enthusiasm. You will be very unhappy if your spouse does not acknowledge God. So spiritually, you must be connected. Don't connect with anybody who's just saying they love the Lord and their actions say something totally different.

About Husbands

Husbands are meant to be the head of the household, led by God to carry out his commands. He gets his commands through the Word of God. This is why it's important that a husband not only be a Christian man, but also a Godly man who prays, reads the Bible, obeys and follows God. To love his wife is to love himself. If he has no experience loving Christ, he has no capacity to love his wife. The Word cleanses and this causes the husband to submit to and follow God. When God is ordering the steps of your husband, you can fall in line with him, stand beside him, be his helpful companion.

If you as a wife are the only one listening to the Holy Spirit and your husband does not have a relationship with God, it is difficult to have peace in your household. Bottom line, you must both have a relationship with God to give love and respect to each other. When you are able to experience and provide those - you are able to walk together in agreement.

Seek Guidance

Seek means to go to God. When you seek something, you are searching it out. Do in-depth study of whatever it is that you are trying to get. You are to seek with a sincere and pure heart, no games. The reason you want to seek and be honest with yourself is so that you can be honest about your own motives.

Is what you want to fill a void? Were you hurt by someone? Did some life experience cause you to want whatever you're in search of? Is there emptiness or loneliness?

Continue Seeking

So many people are married and want to escape their spouse because they chose someone who was not their soul mate. You hear people use the term, "He's not or she's not who I thought," that happens maybe because they sought self-will versus God's will. Perhaps they were impatient, not wanting to wait and hear from God. This "I want it now, got to have it now society," produces poor results and ungodly consequences. Perhaps worse than being impatient is being disobedient, knowing that you are not listening to God but doing it your way. Obedience is better than sacrifice.

Search your motive. God wants relationships. He wants a relationship with you. He has to be the center, it's not an option. When he is the center, he hears, answers and fulfills. He fulfills the heart's desire when you delight yourself in Him. Your destiny is not a mirage.

Intercessory Prayer

Intercessory prayer is an effective and necessary way of communicating directly with God. One of the best things you can do is to pray for others. Because we don't always know who or what we need to pray for, God gives us a direct channel to include everyone in our prayer life through intercessory prayer. As women, we often want to know details and get involved in the tiny little things that may or may not matter. Well, the great thing about intercessory prayer is that you don't have to know a specific issue in order to be effective. If you feel there is a need, it is likely God telling you to take action. When you spend time with Him, he will guide you. You can simply chose a group, category or person and just go from there, because, if something is in your heart or of concern, He likely put it there anyway.

Encouraging Men

The world has changed so much, and so have traditional roles of men and women. It soothed my soul one Saturday when our First Lady brought us together to pray for men. She reminded us to encourage our men. We need them and they need us. In today's society, some of the men are no longer taking their rightful positions as husbands and fathers. In order that they may take the position that God has given them we must not only pray for them, but also intently speak words of life to them. Intercessory prayer is your direct connect.

Sometimes we feel as women that we are the only ones who need healing. There are lots of men who are not working, who are absent in the homes and in the families. They need our prayers. There are mates and spouses who are responsible men but find life tough and situations difficult to navigate. They need our prayers.

We are so used to men being strong. Thus we tend to act like they are machines. We need to give them room to be vulnerable and to heal. As women in relationships, when we have a mate, we may say, "Wow, he's a great provider, he handles his business like a real man should." We want and expect everything out of them. Oftentimes we don't give them room to be vulnerable at all.

As you come in contact with men, speak life into them! Even if they look at you funny use First Lady Dudley's quote: "I thank God for your being a mighty warrior." In sum, you are saying, "I see you as God created you to be." It will make them feel good, you feel good and God will smile too.

Fulfillment is Joy

Freedom is what I now have because of what I know, think and do differently. I know where I am because of what I now see and do differently. My Destiny is not some time in the far off future...every step I take shapes it. When I don't like what I see, I make choices, new choices. I slow down to seek God's guidance and direction then create new thoughts to see myself and my life in a new light.

By being honest and truthful with ourselves, we can live in fullness of joy. If Freedom is your destination, you can find it, if you are willing to search and follow the signs. We must be steadfast and clear about where we are going and then be willing to pay attention along the journey.

I am grateful to God because I learned of Him from an early age. Inside me, though the fear stayed, my awareness of something bigger also stayed. I believe Joy is found through overcoming or rising above the challenging experiences that impact what we think, speak, see, and believe in our heart as truth, and is experienced to the fullest when we have a clear direction of our life's purpose and destiny.

Visible signs fail to convince us to go the "right way" many times because our patterns are set, our habits are formed and our minds are made up. I am grateful that my inability to see did not stop God from staying with me. The "sign" which brings us to faith is the power of God's message to answer the cry of our individual hearts.

When confused, God offers an enlightened mind by faith. When lonely, God offers eternal companionship by faith. When depressed, God offers a reason for joy, by faith. Today, right now, where are you? Are you willing to see beyond the visible signs of what may be lacking, difficult, hurtful, expensive, overwhelming or simply unnecessary?

When you look at where you are and where you want to go, you must have a destination in mind in order to get there. After you figure out where you'd like to be, you can begin to plan your journey. Freedom is found in realizing the boundaries don't really exist. With faith – that there is SOMETHING greater, you can experience fulfillment in the adventure, journey and destination. What you choose to do when you get there is all on you. Going back is easy. Pushing forward is freedom.

Morning Devotion

I need to hear from God. What about you? It is his voice that tells us what he wants us to do and know as a person, as well as how we fit into that entire body – be it church or the home. I cannot function the way God wants me to function if I'm not hearing because my heart is far from him.

It's important to hear and listen as an individual, a family, and team working together in love and unity, in corporate agreement with one another so you may live a harmonious life with everyone, including those on your job.

So think about your household. Who lives with you? Do you take a few moments every day to come to agreement? It's important to be in unity because the head of the household has a vision and will lead you - whether you agree or not, because you are physically there, you are affected. *Freedom in Joy* means getting on the same page and communing with those we live with and are around by embracing them with unconditional love. God can advance your family and your household when you share his good. Do this daily and be lifted.

Joy is Yours!

Freedom is fulfillment. Fulfillment is joy. Joy is yours! It is being all God has called you to be. Freedom in Joy includes your life's purpose. Freedom enjoy your destiny! It's a continuously evolving process which requires your cooperation and awareness. Continually and consistently remind yourself to be grateful while checking your thoughts, attitudes and words.

Chapter 14
Living In Freedom and Joy

My Attitude

My stinking thinking caused me to be afraid to reach out. I was thinking I was going to fail even before I tried. This affected every area of my life because I made excuses, and remained stuck in my own mind. Now my attitude is, "If it doesn't work out, move on, try something else." Just because it doesn't work out doesn't mean you've failed, it just means "that" didn't work out.

My Love for My Husband

Sure, I loved him before, yet I have a deeper love and respect for my husband like never before. I believe it's because God has parted that in me. The deeper I fall in love with God, the closer and deeper I fall in love with him. I'm getting it now. God says how to respect him and how to embrace him, just being the head. Regardless of what choices he makes, I'm his help meet. I am to stand beside him. As the woman, as his gift, I am here to encourage him, to strengthen him, to pray for him and to let him know he can do it.

As women we find it so difficult to be dependent, especially if you were raised like me, to be independent. Submitting to God teaches you how to be dependent on your spouse. Submitting to the will of God is where the freedom comes from. It brings order into your life.

Advancing

No, it's not easy or even simple, if it's not your habit however, don't stop. Get up every day ready to start again with new thoughts. Greatness is in you and greatness is in me because God put it there. He put it there not for it to lie dormant, but to take action and charge in walking in your greatness. Trust! Have Faith! Rejoice in your new path! You have been re-shaped and reborn to live in your destiny!

You see when your mindset and your thoughts began to unite and harmonize with what's in your heart then you begin to speak into existence the very thing that has always been impregnated inside of you...your destiny.

And you, in turn, are speaking the language of those new thoughts that are planted in your heart. That's joy. Negative thinking never gives you the opportunity to take your feet off the brakes at the green light. You realize this is your past. Your past had passed so fill up the tank with new thoughts. Pay attention to and recognize when it is half full and fill up again. Don't wait until it gets empty again. That's reliving your past. You can't afford to go backward when you clearly know what lies ahead. You must keep moving forward.

Every day remind yourself of where you're going and how you're going to get there and bring others along with you. This is freedom. On top with a different view is joy. Creating continuous moments of gratitude for each life experience you journey along the path is Freedom in Joy.

Someone is waiting on you and counting on you. Give to them the love and hope which were given to you so they can journey into their destiny. Pass the "joy" stick to others so they too can move forward. Forgive yourself. Wake up! Get up! Get Growing! Let go! Let God!

Here are some ways you can journey along the Path to Freedom. The journey itself is a process to help you gain freedom, stay free through joy. You don't have to limit yourself to this process only. You will surely discover more along your way. But this is a great start!

The Path to Freedom is a Process

The path to freedom is a process. The process is necessary so you have clear signs to keep you focused and on the right path to your destiny. You can get to Freedom in Joy by stepping outside your circumstances and situations and looking at them in a different way, from a different perspective. That is, the view from within your heart. It's just like my experience at the monument Gateway Arch. I made a conscious decision to change my position from the outside space where I was standing below, risk going inside then taking a ride up in this 63 stories monument until I had reached the very top. Why? My heart desired not just a glimpse of the arch from the outside, but a better view from the inside. As you walk the path to Freedom, believe and see yourself at the top.

1) Reading the Bible

God's Word strengthens and empowers us, uplifts and encourages us to press, push, and praise in all circumstances. So RISE up and TAKE your stand TODAY. Take possession of what's already yours - peace, healing, rest, deliverance, trust, hope, finances...
Give thanks in all circumstances; for this is God's will for you in Christ Jesus.   I Thessalonians 5:18

2) Prayerful Living

Dear friend, I pray that you may enjoy good health and that all may go well with you, even as your soul is getting along well.
"Say to him: 'Long life to you! Good health to you and your household!"   3 John 1:2

3) Knowing You Were Born to Prosper

"For I know the plans I have for you," declares the Lord, "plans to prosper you and not to harm you, plans to give you hope and a future.   Jeremiah 29:11

4) Believing Miracles Still Happen

Do you believe in miracles? Miracles do still happen although many don't believe this. When we begin to walk in the power and authority God has given us - IT IS A MIRACLE! Your MIRACLE is Your DESTINY. Your DESTINY is Your Miracle.

5) Understanding You Were Born to Shine

Think Daily: *I know my life is not an event. It didn't just happen. It's about my creation - my God experience.*

GOD SAID Let us make man in our image, after our likeness. So God created man in his own image, in the image of God created he him. Can't you see the REFLECTION? We are created in the Glory of GOD. GOD SAID - A LIGHT IS BORN!

6) Activating Your Faith

Your Faith has built up your resistance - Your immune- to fight against the tactics of the enemy says the Lord. … Do not look back - the old nature is no more. You have become new creatures in me.

7) Trusting, believing and remaining faithful, even when your faith is tested.

Say to yourself: *I'm moving forward. I mean it, seek it, live through it.*

8) Godly Love, Unity and Harmony with Yourself and Others

Affirm: *I will continue to hear and submit to God. I will pour God's love into all who will freely receive. Love never fails. I will love The Lord with all my heart, soul, and strength. With ALL of me.*

"Let me give you a new command: Love one another. In the same way I loved you, you love one another. This is how everyone will recognize that you are my disciples-when they see the love you have for each other.

John 13:34-35 MSG

9) Rising Up and Moving Forward With A Plan in Hand

The manifestation of the Spirit is given to EVERY man to profit together at the same time. ALL must WORK! ALL must GO! THERE ARE NO BENCHWARMERS IN THE KINGDOM OF GOD. People are waiting on us. People are counting on us. People are dying in their spirit, body, and soul. We must win lost souls no matter the cost. We must advance the Kingdom of God for His name sake. We ALL must GO! Lord Thy will be done in earth as IT IS in heaven. Amen and Amen.

10) Standing Boldly

Repeat, Repeat, Repeat: "I Don't Shrink! We Don't Shrink!" I don't faint! I push FORWARD! We don't shrink! We GO FORWARD! Amen and Amen.

11) Understanding What Held You Captive, Staying Free

To walk in your destiny, you must know what it is. Forget about what others think. Forget about whether or not you're going to fail. You can't get to another level if you can't see for yourself, trust, believe, step out on faith, and acknowledge destiny is yours. Once you know and understand, there aren't any excuses for going backward. You must stay focused and continue moving forward. Just as you have grown physically into an adult, there is no going back in time to being a child physically again. Only your mindset and thoughts take you back into childish thinking and childish ways of doing and being. Every day you must grow and mature in your thought process. The old is gone.

The new has come - be free.

Chapter 15
I Am Free Poem

I AM FREE

I am free, no longer bound by the cares of this world because Jesus' blood covers me.

No more chains are holding me - for God's love and mercy embrace me.

I am free because of God's faithfulness and promises to me.

You shall live and not die; I come to give you LIFE and that more ABUNDANTLY.

I choose to LIVE. I choose to be free. I choose to love me because…God loves me and he cares. He cares enough to protect and rescue me.

He rescue by uprooting the thoughts planted in my mind to damage and destroy me.

I am free to trust God with my life. I yield and give him all of me.

All or nothing! ALL means all and NOTHING means nothing.

I am free to behold the Lamb of God so that I may LIVE AGAIN.

Reborn! Restored! Resurrected! I have been REVIVED to live again!

I am free from the wounds that have scarred me.

Because God said I am healed by his stripes, and not the stripes of past history.

Free from everything that caused my spirit man to die, even in the spring.

Everything that I am – my entire being is free.

Because God said whom he sets free is free indeed.

I AM free indeed to release ALL the past hurts, pain, and sufferings in exchange for joy, laughter, hope, peace, and a fulfilling future.

I am free to let go of ALL the burdens of life I have carried beyond delivery. Yes, I am free to rejoice; shed tears of JOY for I have finally found me.

I have finally found my voice and can now walk...WHOLE and HOLY with strength and authority. Praise the Lord I am free to be me. I surrender my will to God and declare my freedom. I declare my LIBERTY!

I AM FREE. Yes! Free to give myself fully and completely – I surrender ALL of me.

I permit God to take charge over my life, for I am persuaded and convinced my life, His purpose and His plan for me is for REAL -- not a MIRAGE.

I now live a joyful life and rest in the promises which have been spoken over me. I am healed and delivered! FREE!

Oh, I am free.   I don't have to hide the praise inside of me.

The storm has passed over. The battle has been fought and won.

I AM free because God has made me free.

My lips sing praises and my feet walk victoriously for I AM living in my destiny!

Lavanda Rochelle Heard

Christ has set us free to live a free life. So take your stand!
Never again let anyone put a harness of slavery on you.
Galatians 5:1 The Message Bible

A Note From the Publisher

Mission Possible Press...

Creating Legacies through Absolute Good Works

As a publisher, I have the opportunity to transform hopeful writers into successful authors. This brings me great pleasure because I believe everyone has wisdom to share and valuable stories to tell.

Rochelle, as I call her, (Lavanda's middle name), is an amazing woman with a kind heart, powerful intuition and insightful wisdom. Working with her has been an adventurous experience which I absolutely know was a gift from God. Did I mention she's a prayer warrior? Get to know her and I'm sure you'll get texts in the middle of the night as well!

I am honored and pleased to present this book, *Freedom in Joy, My Destiny Is Not a Mirage,* written by Lavanda Rochelle as part of our Extraordinary Living Series.

In the Spirit of Communication,

Jo Lena Johnson, Founder and Publisher
Mission Possible Press,
A division of Absolute Good
AbsoluteGood.com
MissionPossiblePress.com

About the Author

Lavanda Rochelle Heard was born in East St. Louis, Illinois and raised in the neighboring community known as "Park Side" in Centreville, Illinois. She is the sixth child of eight siblings. Rochelle and her husband Paul of 25 years have two sons, Joshua and Joseph, and currently reside in the state of Illinois as a retired United States Air Force family. She has accompanied her husband on his overseas military and civilian assignments in Europe and the Middle East.

Rochelle has earned three college degrees, an A.A. and B.S. from Chapman University, in California and an A.S. from Keiser College in Florida graduating with honors of Magna Cum Laude. Additionally, she holds a Child Development Associate (CDA) National Credential with the Council for Professional Recognition in Washington DC, and is an Illinois Board of Education State and No Child Left Behind – (NCLB) Approved Para-professional and an AmeriCorps Alumnus.

At the age of 11, Rochelle gave her life to Christ. Every since her childhood, she has had a deep desire to please God by being a willing vessel in the earth, serving both God and mankind.

Rochelle loves working with children. After 9 ½ years of hands on experience in her degree field of technology working for the Aerospace Corporation in both California and Florida, she discovered her true passion and purpose of genuinely assisting others, having mercy and showing compassion towards others. Thus, she transitioned from the computer world to the education world to allow herself more opportunities to "help others" and "encourage others." The majority of her life's career from that time forward revolved around caring for and meeting the needs of families and their children through various educational institutions and childcare services, to include her very own home daycare business "Kids of Character" closing after 7 years for her family move to the Middle East. She diligently and wholeheartedly provided services on behalf of non-challenged children and challenged children having physical, learning and behavioral disabilities. She also served for Military Base Chapel Services and other community churches where God planted her family during their family relocations to other states and while overseas.

Now as a member of New Life in Christ Interdenominational Church (NLICIC) in O'Fallon, Illinois since 2004, Rochelle devotes her time serving in the ministry as a team Greeter and Minister in Training. She has recently joined a team of intercessors at NLICIC called Project Graduation "SFI" Special Forces Intercessors who pray through the District 189 East St. Louis, Illinois schools. Prior to these ministries at NLICIC, she served faithfully as a Pre-K to Kindergartener teacher from 2005 to 2009.

www.ingramcontent.com/pod-product-compliance
Lightning Source LLC
La Vergne TN
LVHW021538080426
835509LV00019B/2720